Why Did the Ancient Greeks Become a Seafaring People?

Jacques Pierre

Why Did the Ancient Greeks Become a Seafaring People?

Reflective History

Editing: Le Club d'Aventure d'Outre-Mer
Proof Reading: Le Club d'Aventure d'Outre-Mer

Front Page Art: hotpot.ai

Publisher: BoD – Books on Demand, Hellerup, Denmark

Printer: BoD – Books on Demand, Norderstedt, Germany

ISBN: 978-87-43055-402

INTRODUCTION

The question that is the title to this book might as well have been set to any seafaring people in the past. seafaring is a very costly and dangerous venture, especially when it has not been established already.

So why incur the risk of this endeavor? It all comes down to a question of need. When there is a need to be covered, there usually will be found a way to cover it.

Ancient Greece was not able to cover all its needs internally as it developed, so it needed to import them.

One might say that whether a need will be covered is dependent on whether it outweighs the costs, which is correct, but as the need of the Greeks of many of the ancient city states was for grain to feed themselves the need was rather pressing.

So, the ancient Greeks set sail to find extra sources of base foods.

Alongside this then came other needed materials, the bronze and the wood for the ships themselves.

When the goods that are needed are base foods then the risk quickly becomes less important. Stable foods are simply needed and exports to exchange for the produce will be found in one way or the other. The only alternative is population decline.

The Greek population did not decline but expanded, so both the seafaring skills and export goods to exchange for food imports were developed.

The Greeks had the good fortune of proximity to large and highly developed cultures that could be reached by sea.

Furthermore, they also had less developed areas with a grain surplus in close proximity. These areas which included the northern Black Sea region imported goods from more developed regions, which they traded for grain, fur and amber. The desired goods were often metalworks and ceramics.

The Greeks would thus also maintain profitable transit trade between developed cultures of Egypt and the Middle East and Europe.

This was a result of the fortunate geographical position of Greece being situated between these regions.

Especially during the Bronze age where metal production was very complex the raw material was transported far to the metal works and were only produced in a few places. This led to bronze being shipped far and wide to the areas that could not produce it, which often flowed through Greece.

Although the iron age led to more dispersed metal production more refined metal works were still exported from the developed cultures in the Middle East to Europe and Greece continued to maintain a favorable position in this trade due to its location in between. Thus, Greece had a favorable position to evolve a maritime culture.

But it was not only the favorable location of Greece that made the sea trade possible.

Greece itself also lent a number of factors to the Greeks, which made a strong maritime development more likely.

THE LANDSCAPE

It can actually be the land of a country itself that makes a turn to the sea natural.

Greece is a collection of islands and peninsulas with many fjords cutting in between. On land high mountains rise up and cut off connection between the short river valleys, where most Greeks settled. These river valleys and other lowlands are very disconnected making it difficult to transport goods between them. With ancient means of transportation, it is very limited how much can be transported over land. You are limited to what you or a beast of burden can carry or what can fit is a cart.

On water, however, even a simple raft can carry way more mass and volume than anything on land. Add to this that weight is much easier to push on water and it becomes clear how water connected and land divided.

Given the curly nature of Greece many areas could be reached when sailing and the islands could only be reached over water.

This made the sea a natural choice in Greece. Compared to land area it has a formidable length of coast and the densest populated areas are all by the sea.

Compare this to Egypt where all of the country is folded around the Nile and everything can be reached along the Nile. Although there is an access out by the river delta there is not much reason to reach out beyond the delta and mostly it was not necessary as both the Greeks and Phoenicians came to the Egyptians to trade rather than the Egyptians needing to go out.

This is very much due to the richness of Egypt. It had much to offer and so others came, while the Greeks needed to go out, because they did not have the same richness in their own land.

The shape of Greece also led to the political structure with independent city states. The mountains created barriers that made it difficult to create large centralized societies. So, each small region had internal self-governance.

This did not mean that they could not be part of larger unions, but the Greek states continually turned towards self-governance.

This was easy to do as the landscape provided a large degree of protection.

Athens became the Greek city state with the strongest dominance, which was achieved through its large navy that could control the seaways between the different areas of Greece. And a navy was needed to maintain power further away in Greece.

Athens did not maintain control by having troops in the other city states but by dominating the connection between them.

And this is an important note about a naval empire. It maintains control by controlling the seaways through which trade flows rather than directly controlling the land.

Greece was perfectly shaped for this kind of control rather than land control.

With each area of Greece forming its own small state they also each followed their own goals sailing out to best provide the needs of their state.

As there was competition between each state especially if there was close proximity, it was difficult to expand in the closest region, so each city state could send ships out to find easier markets than the closest area.

THE SEASCAPE

It is not only the landscape that is important for the development of maritime culture, but also the sea that surrounds this landscape.

And surround is the correct word, when it comes to Greece. All the islands and peninsulas make for a land completely surrounded by the sea.

Most other ancient civilizations were land and river based. With many areas very four from the sea.

This is not the case in Greece. The country consists of so many islands and peninsulas that everywhere is reasonably close to the sea. The only limiting factor being that the Aegean peninsula blocks access east west necessitating going south around this main peninsula, which in ancient times could be treacherous.

When talking about a seascape it is not just the water surface that is important but also the entire region beneath the surface. This includes the underwater landscape, which is often a continuation of the landscape above the water.

In Greece this means that the mountains and valleys above the waves are also found beneath the waves, with many mountain tops and ridges forming the islands of the Aegean Sea.

Many mountain tops also do not break the surface of the water forming reefs that are a danger to ships.

This is not just a bad thing, however, as subsurface cliffs and mountains form good conditions for marine life-giving Greece good fishing waters in ancient times.

Thus, a large part of the locally available food stuff for the ancient Greeks came from their waters, which were significantly richer than the land.

Fishing was therefore an important activity in the city states and when people have fishing as their livelihood, they naturally become accustomed to the sea.

Indeed, in ancient times the Greek often viewed Thalassa, the sea, as more their homeland than the inland civilizations that they visited in the east.

The strong variation in the subsurface landscape of the Greek seascape also meant that Greek sailors became accustomed to difficult waters and knew how subsurface structures or even above surface land affected the currents. Meaning they had a good ability to read the sea even when far from home.

Knowing the current and anticipating them is very important even today and even more so in an age of oars and simple sails.

If you know the currents then you can also ride them to reach a destination with less effort. Riding it when it goes where you want to go and returning when it Turns. All this comes with experience with the waters.

Tides are also important here. How large is the difference? When do they come and where do they allow you to go? Often you can ride the tide just like a current to get where you want to go. And you also need to know the tide, if it is the only thing raising the water high enough for you to pass an area by boat.

All these things affect the Aegean Sea with all its twists and turns making for an excellent region for sailors to learn the trade.

Another important factor of the Greek seascape is where it connects with the landscape. The shape and geography of the country blesses it with a large number of natural harbors. This is important as many areas of the world lacks many natural harbors thus impending the access to the sea. but Greece has them in abundance and can thus access the sea easily with even larger vessels.

Natural harbors are important not just to have somewhere to access land to and from the ships, but just as important it allows for ships to be launched.

Furthermore, natural harbors along the coast also offer important protection from the sea. Rough waters are dangerous for any ship and in ancient times the sea could be very dangerous due to the limits of the vessels. Thus, it was very important to be able to seek shelter, when the waters became rough.

So even if a natural harbor was not used to make a settlement, it could still be important as a spot where ships could be anchored for a time both to avoid rough weather, but also if a fleet was to be assembled from many places.

The Greek seascape has all of these things in abundance thus making it well suited for maritime activity.

Thus, the Greek homeland offered excellent conditions for the development of a strong maritime culture that would reach out across the Mediterranean.

This was only further supported by Greece's location around the middle of the Mediterranean and at the only access point to the Black Sea.

The ancient Greeks thus had a good starting point for the development of a strong maritime culture only really countered by their competitors in the levant; The Phoenicians, who were a row of city states in short river valleys along the coast of the Levant. Their strength was their position directly between the advanced cultures in the Middle East and the Mediterranean Sea.

The locations of these two maritime cultures led to the Phoenicians mainly spreading along the southern coast of the Mediterranean, while the Greeks spread mostly along the northern coast.

Both mainly trailed along the coastlines as the open sea was dangerous where no land could be reached fairly quickly at the other side.

The seascape thus formed the routes that would be taken from one place to another heavily influenced by another factor: The weather!

THE WINDS

Salling is the process of traveling along at the surface, where the atmosphere and hydrosphere touch. Thus, sailing utilizes the forces that are created from this. The most well-known of these is using the winds to gain momentum, while being buoyant in the water.

The ancient Greeks as well as the other seagoing cultures used oars and human muscle to propel their vessels especially when going against the flows and winds, but by using the winds, it is possible to move with much less manpower, which was especially useful, when keeping down costs.

A simple square rig was used to propel the vessel in the wind. This meant that the vessels were limited in their maneuverability and had to wait for the right conditions to reach its goal.

The Mediterranean region had great advantages, when using simple square rigs. This was its wind conditions during summer.

Under the hot summer sun, the land area heats up and creates strong updrafts that lead to constant onshore winds during the day. Meaning you can ride the wind in.

Vice versa the land cools fast during night while the water retains more heat. Thus, updraft moves to the water and downdraft to land meaning you can ride the wind to sea in the evening, night and early morning.

This made ancient navigation and sailing by wind a waiting game, where you came to harbor during the day and left in evening.

Aside from this the knowledge of tides and currents would also be used to go, where you wanted, but the onshore and offshore winds were a constant during the summer.

Not quite so during the winter where storms and larger weather patterns made sailing far more dangerous.

So, the Summer was the season for maritime trade and distant sailing.

During this season a ship could sail from an island in the evening or early morning and ride the offshore winds out to sea and then when reaching another island or the mainland could use the onshore wind of the day to enter harbor. This was quite a useful set of conditions for the use of sails.

This could also be done for simple hopping along the coastline. Again, a ship could set out with the offshore wind of early morning and go out as far as needed and then when the wind turned could go in with the onshore wind of the day further along the coast.

Since going in would always be at day a further advantage was that the light of day would be there when entering the harbor giving much needed visibility.

The Mediterranean weather also has the added summer bonus of not being prone to fog thus giving a high certainty of having good visibility. One of the things that the Greeks feared when going to the Black Sea and especially the Northern coasts was the fog that could manifest in these regions and thus blinding the ships to what lay ahead.

This was a problem that the Greeks did not suffer under in the summer season of their homeland. Also, the greater Mediterranean basin is usually spared from fog during summer making it well suited for maritime activity.

The weather of ancient Greece thus supported great conditions for the development of maritime activity, because the weather was generally calm during summer and had the predictable daily shift between onshore and offshore winds.

In situations where the winds were not favorable oars could be used if enough men were onboard, but for trade where the cost of manpower was a concern, it would often be cheaper to wait for the right conditions.

But when enough manpower sailed out with the ship, it was possible to shift from wind power to manpower and thus gain much stronger maneuverability against the winds and currents. This would especially be the case for naval vessels or armed merchant vessels for longer journeys to foreign lands, where protection was needed.

The conditions were dominant during the summer, which was thus the sailing season. The storms of winter were dangerous for the vessels and the wind patterns of summer with regular onshore and offshore winds change due to the colder weather and diminished sunlight.

Therefore, by far the most maritime activity was during the summer, while winter was mostly reduced to coastal fishing to maintain the local supply of fish.

Most routes were thus of a distance that could be traveled to and from within the sailing season. If a route was greater than could be traveled within the season then the winter could he stayed out at the destination with a return trip in the following season making the trip dual season or more.

Such multi seasonal journeys required the goods traded to bet of great value or simply being to a colony where staying was easy.

Most routes in the Mediterranean did not require more than one season, however, and especially not in the highly developed Eastern Mediterranean.

The Greeks thus had a season determined by the weather, where the maritime activity was centered, but during this season large scale maritime activity was possible in order to reach the areas where the Greeks would trade for the goods that they needed.

The Greeks thus had a set of regional conditions that affected their development into a maritime culture. This was heavily influenced by the sea being the easiest path to reach the other developed cultures in the Middle East and Egypt.

The conditions being mentioned until now have been the landscape, the seascape and the atmosphere that together make up the environment.

THE ENVIRONMENT

The Mediterranean is an enclosed sea with the land around it and mountains rising up inland.

This gave rise to the saying that the Greeks were around the Mediterranean like frogs around a pond. And this is an important note that when sailing in the Mediterranean you are going somewhere. You are going towards land.

The winds, currents and the position of Greece within the Mediterranean and the fact that the more developed cultures were easiest to reach over water made it reasonable for the Greeks to set sail further away from the Aegean home sea.

The Levant and Egypt could be reached by trailing the Southern coast of Anatolia without going further to sea.

That is not to say that other routes were not used, only that trailing the coast was a path to each of these areas.

Here they would also reach the only other serious maritime culture of the time; The Phoenicians.

Another condition of the environment that would also greatly affect both Greek and Phoenician trade and even contact over the sea was the geology.

Metallurgy requires having access to the needed metals, The bronze age was the first era where specific resources were searched far afield.

The bronze age is an excellent example of early international commodity trade. Bronze was primarily produced in the near east. Bronze is an alloy of copper and tin, so both metals are needed to produce the metal. Although copper is readily available in the near east and Cyprus. Tin is much more rare and where available is bound in hazardous arsenic compounds.

Better and much more abundant sources of tin can be found in the western Mediterranean on the European side. That is what is today Spain, France, Italy and all the way to Britain.

Tin being the smaller fraction of the bronze alloy being about 12,5% tin to 87.5% copper meant that only small amounts of tin would need to be brought back to create large amounts of bronze. Some of which could then be brought west to exchange for tin.

This very early commodity trade was dominated by the Phoenicians given their position on the coast next to the major bronze cultures.

However, Greece was directly en route to the sources of tin, which meant that the Greeks, who already had a local maritime culture became heavily influenced by the more developed Phoenicians so far as to also become a maritime culture in the Mediterranean and being heavily influenced by the advanced bronze culture and becoming one of the true bronze civilizations, of the bronze age adapting the advanced centralized and literate government structures of the bronze age near east.

The culture being presented in Homer's Iliad is this palace culture of the bronze age capable of mounting a large fleet from all the Greek states under king Agamemnon. The size of this fleet is an indication of the maritime nature of even bronze age Greece.

Thus, Greece's location and the geology of surrounding areas with tin deposits to the west and copper deposits and bronze production to the east gave Greece a favorable position to develop into a maritime trade hub. In time they also sailed tin and bronze from place to place in competition with the Phoenicians.

Greece's own geology also gave certain advantages, having many deposits of clay making it a hub for the production and export of pottery giving the Greeks something to trade for other goods.

Furthermore, Greece has deposits of iron and silver, which became important in the iron age.

Many of the early Greek settlements outside Greece proper and in Magna Graecia, today Southern Italy, were most likely ports along the tin trade routes where the ships would rest safely before continuing.

With the collapse of the bronze age and the turmoil, which led into the iron age much of the tin and bronze trade network ceased to be, but Greece would still have pottery, iron and silver to exchange for other goods, meaning that even with the fall of the centralized bronze age palace cultures the Greek maritime trade culture would remain, but now more devoted to exchanging Greek products for needed goods from the outside than being a transit point for an international trade network. Much of Greek settlement ended up happening in the archaic iron age period between the end of the bronze age and the classical period.

The end of the bronze age also led to a major population shift in Greece with the Dorian Greeks moving down the Peloponnesian peninsula and the Ionians moving out to the islands and to the coastal regions of Lydia, which is today the western coast of Turkey.

This period also led to an expansion in the Greek colonization of the Mediterranean. Many settlements were established in Magna Graecia, today Southern Italy.

Many of these settlements had the function of being trading posts, where the mother city then could sail to in order to safely conduct trade into the hinterland. Much of this would have been built on earlier connections from trade routes of the bronze age. The goals for the Greeks were still to maintain supply of necessary goods to the home towns.

This also became much more pressing with the end of the Mycenean bronze age palace state as the centralized state was broken into small self-governing entities that had to supply their own needs.

Furthermore, the new polis states were very competitive with each other. Thus, often they would not trade directly with each other, but independently trade with more distant areas that were not part of the internal Greek competition.

This all merely fueled the maritime activity as the individual Greek polis states blocked each other's options for meeting their needs in the homeland.

Athens is a great example of this being isolated on the peninsula of Attica with hostile city states blocking the peninsula leaving only the sea as a means to reach out and get the much-needed supply of grain.

Athens thus maintained a large navy and had a force in the geology of Attica, which sported both great resources of clay and even more importantly silver in the Laurian mines.

Athens also painstakingly built up an olive oil production in Attica, which became another source of exchange.

This olive oil production did have a downside, however, as it further limited the food crops produced in Attica making Athens even more dependent on grain imports and thus dependent on the navy and merchant marine without which Athens would starve.

It is further interesting that by the classical era Greece had become dependent on imported wood to build its ships meaning they became even more dependent on their trade network to maintain their resources.

This meant that financing the system became even more important.

In this case the Laurean mines and their rich silver veins became very important to Athens as silver was a sought-after metal that quickly came to finance the merchant marine of the city state.

Especially as the silver started to be minted. It most likely started as a way of showing that it was Athenian silver, but this marking came to mean that the coins would be used as a certain means of exchange, because its value was independent of state decree. It was the trust that Athenian silver was pure that was important and thus the first real currency came into being through the trade system of Athens further fueling the development of Greek sea trade.

A further important development of the classical period was the establishment of the Persian empire, which swallowed up the Phoenicians. They became subjects of Persia, which meant that they had to supply the Persian navy with ships and could monopolize trade on the Persian subject states, but limited their rights to trade outside the empire, cutting them off from their daughter cities like Cartage.

The Greeks thus gained less competition from the Phoenicians in the parts of the Mediterranean outside of Persian influence limiting competitions to the areas, where Carthage had influence.

This gave the Greeks a large sphere of influence, where they were the only real sea merchants. This was a boon for a society like the Greek, which had such a great need for imports of basic goods like grain.

It is important to note that the Greeks did not establish colonies due to imperial ambitions, but as a means to facilitate trade and to have safe havens for the ships en route to their port of call. The colonies were for a large part trading stations that grew because the trade was good. The original settlers were thus emporoi, traders, and the colonies, emporion, trading places or markets.

A trading station would be set up in an area, where trade could be established with the local population in the hinterland, when they had something of value to trade in. By having a permanent trading station in the area, the Greek ships knew where to go and would be greeted by compatriots. Thus, only the first expedition to an area would go to unknown territory.

By having the trading station that when successful would evolve into a colony the mother city would have a trading partner in the area that could receive the ships and make trade in the area across the year. Thus, the colony would function as a depot for trade.

Thus, the trade would not need to be conducted all at once with the local population.

The Greeks thus sought out their extended environment for areas that had resources they lacked to trade with the goods they had. This also meant that a colony would often be placed in an area that had both what the mother city wanted and where the local population wanted what the Greek mother city could offer.

The Athenians gained a great advantage in this as their silver coins became a sought commodity in and of themselves, which had the effect that they did not establish many colonies as such, because their coins easily facilitated trade without these.

This is not to say that they did not have trading stations; merely that her silver drachm gave an advantage and they often used the colonies of their partner cities in the Delian League.

Athens thus had a great advantage in the geology of its environment that heavily influenced its ability to establish a large maritime presence.

It is important to note that the Greek city states were not empire builders. They established their trading networks and colonies to cover the needs of their city state that could not be covered by its immediate environment.

Actually, the city states were the opposite of empire builders using significant resources on avoiding any attempt at establishing a centralized government to the extent that the lesser city states would group together to quell any city state becoming too powerful.

This disunity meant that much had to be brought in across the sea and that some Greek city states would rather trade with barbarians than with each other.

The classical Greeks thus had a cultural environment that was inherently separatist and splittist.

Also, the colonies and daughter cities established by the Greeks as they reached out across the sea might have been historically and culturally bonded to the mother city, but they were not subject to the mother city. Greek colonial cities were independent entities that could operate independently. They usually stayed connected to the mother city and were expected to retain contact, but the mother city would rarely have any ability to control the daughter city.

This does make sense, when one remembers the large distances between mother city and daughter city and the difficulty in maintaining stable contact. Ships would go to and thro as it was possible not necessarily as was wanted. It was thus only natural that a daughter city would be fully self-governing as it would mostly need to deal with its own problems. The mother and daughter cities could lend each other support in times of crisis, however, and often did so, but always were limited by the ability to send aid once notified of the need. Furthermore, it could also happen that mother and daughter cities found each other on opposite sides in a conflict.

Thus, the Greek colonies were not really parts of an empire and were only culturally unified. The concept of a colonial empire was not really one that existed among the Greeks and it really is something that the eyes of later observers has inferred unto the Greeks when comparing with the Romans.

What the daughter cities did was the most important thing when going out to sea. They gave the ships somewhere meaningful to go. Any voyage needs to be done for a reason, even if the reason is just leisure. And the Greeks went out to get something that was available somewhere else to bring it back to the home city. And for this having a culturally close daughter city was perfect. It provided a great deal of security in making the voyage safe, predictable and profitable! All things that were often sorely lacking in the ancient world. It is nice to have some where to go, where people speak your language and have almost the same customs.

Thus, the Greek city states established a disparate network of daughter cities across the Mediterranean connected by the sea and separated by the land and with each mother city having its own set of daughter cities.

From the Greek viewpoint the world was a rim of land around the Mediterranean and Black Sea that they reached across water rather than land. This is not to say that the Greeks did not know of the Atlantic or the great Eurasian inland, they did, but the world they knew and dealt with was the one described.

Generally, the maritime part of this world was more or less divided with the Greeks dominating the northern parts and the Phoenicians the Southern. In the middle they met in areas like the Iberian Peninsula and Sicily and the Greeks operated in Cyrenaica near Egypt and both had controlled trading access to Pharaonic Egypt. The Greeks through the trading post Naucratis that was allowed by the Pharaoh.

Given the Greek's natural geographic tilt to the north of the Mediterranean two important natural passages were defining for the Greeks access to the seas.

One was the Bosporus strait that is the only water connection to the Black Sea meaning that any ships going to or from the Black Sea would need to pass through the Aegean Sea even if the Bosporus was not controlled by the Greeks themselves as was the case when the Persian Empire controlled the strait. This made the Black Sea an obvious area of Greek activity.

The other is actually a land Passage that had great importance for sea transport. This was the Corinthian isthmus that connects The Peloponnese peninsula to the rest of the Greek mainland. On one side is the Gulf of Corinth going west to the Ionian Sea and the Adriatic and on the other the Saronic Gulf opening to the east.

This isthmus was an important spot for transporting goods across to avoid the dangerous waters south around the Peloponnese.

This made the four city states at the isthmus very wealthy and powerful. They were Corinth and Sicyon on the western side and Megara and Aegina on the island of the same name to the east.

This Isthmus gave the Greeks a great short cut from east to west.

The Isthmus also, represented the geographical center of the core lands with Sparta to the south in Peloponnese, Thebes just to the north in Boeotia and Athens to the south east next to the Saronic Gulf.

The Isthmus thus was a major connecting point in the Greek world that could be reached from all sides. It also was a center area between the two major colonization areas of the Ionian coast of Asia minor to the east and Magna Grecia in Southern Italy and Sicily. These two regions had a junction at the Corinthian isthmus.

Corinth indeed was also mother city to the most successful city in Magna Grecia and indeed one of the most successful Greek cities in classical antiquity; Syracuse on Sicily, which would outshine its mother city and compete with Athens at its zenith as the largest and most populous Greek city state.

Corinth thus had a very strong position to dominate the sea trade, which brought it into conflict with the rising power of Athens.

Athens through the Delian league came to dominate the Eastern Greek regions along the Ionian coast and importantly the Bosporus and thus the connection to the Black Sea and the grain supply there.

The location of Athens on the peninsula of Attica next to the Corinthian Isthmus and the Saronic gulf meant that the growing naval power of Athens brought it into conflict with Corinth, Megara and the island of Aegina, which would break all Greek unity.

The geography of Greece itself thus created both internal conflict and outward expansion to supply the needs of the city states.

This also made the Greek mercenary, Greeks were often employed as mercenaries in other lands like Egypt and even the Persian empire, which the Greeks had thought against, but the city states would often ally with the Persians against other city states accepting the rich fortunes that the Persians could offer.

This is another indicator of the very splittist nature of the ancient Greek civilization. Each city state thought to secure the supplies that they needed in competition with the other states.

There was no clear divide between the areas that the city states would establish daughter cities in. Syracuse was a daughter city of Corinth, which could be reached from the Gulf of Corinth in a rather straightforward manner.

This needed not be the case, however as Phocaea on the coast of Asia Minor somewhat south of the Dardanelles would establish Massalia, Now Marseille is France, Emporion, now Empuries in Spain, and Elea, now Velia in Italy. Quite far from the mother city, but sensible as Phocaea traded in Tin for the production of Bronze and these areas, where sources of Tin. In the case of Massalia it arrived all the way from Britain, showing the extent of the trade networks in 600 BC, when Massalia was founded.

The Greeks thus established themselves in areas that could supply much needed resources either to cover their own direct needs or to trade on for other products that they needed. Like is common for outwards reaching cultures this is highly grounded in the lacking of the home environment to cover the needs of the population. If an area is rich in resources the work I the population will tend to be focused inward, whereas a culture with an environment lacking in resources especially foods will tend to reach outward to cover this need through trade or theft.

When reaching out the Greeks would then try to seek out a harbor area for settlement that would have very similar conditions to their homeland. That is a good natural harbor, a defensible hill of mountain for the Acropolis to seek shelter from attacks and some farmland to cover the essentials.

A much sought after requirement for a settlement would be good fishing grounds especially for tuna, which was a highly sought after supplement for the diet.

The Greeks thus always sought conditions, where their technology would fit the conditions. An important requirement would thus be that the settlement's coastal condition would be favorable to the galley type ships that were used in the Mediterranean during antiquity and beyond.

THE VESSELS AND SHIPS

Any vessels and seacrafts are always entirely dependent on the resources available to the builders. A boat or ship will be built based simply on what is available to build from. Add to that the knowledge of what can be built from the available materials.

This fast makes the limits of Greek naval technology clear. The ancient Greek era fell in the bronze age and iron age making both metals available. Iron is susceptible to rust in saltwater, however, severely limiting what it could be used for on any given ship.

Aside from that these metals were valuable and would only be used in a limited fashion, where needed on any given ship.

What was available for the building of boats, ships and other seacrafts was wood, rope, cloth, skin and tar. Tar would be made from wood through the production of charcoal or imported from areas where tarpits existed. Rope and cloth could be made from plant fiber or wool. Skin was made from hides of animals.

These were the basic and primary products available for the manufacture of ships. Wood was used for the production of the ship's hull. Often with a method called mortise and tenon. Basically, the mortises were holes in the planks that would make up the hull. The planks would then be fitted together with tenons that fitted into the mortises. Smaller holes in the planks would connect to the side of the mortises through which dowels would then be hammered into similar holes on the tenons locking the planks in place.

The hull would then have all small openings filled out with tar to make it waterproof allowing it to float without taking in water.

Mast and oars would similarly be cut from wood and the mast locked in place with a larger version of dowels. Ropes would be used for rigging that held the sail and since the mast was often made to be raised and lowered the rigging also held the most aloft.

Rope would also be used to move the ship in port and to bind the cargo in place.

Like the wooden hull the rope for the rigging would also be cured with tar to make it withstand the weather and water.

Cloth would be used to make the said. Wool would be a favored material for the large sail cloth that would catch the wind. The sail would be secured to the boom and mast with rope.

Skin could be used for the hull of small skin boats and for shin covers on larger vessels.

An important extra use for skin would be as freshwater containers onboard. Fresh water is necessary for the crews, when traveling on the salty waters of the Mediterranean.

Of the materials needed for ship building the ancient Greeks had skin and wood from the sheep and goats grazing the mountain slopes of the country. So, these were available.

Wood and lumber were a larger problem. Greece did and does have forests, but the country had early been deforested with only light forestation remaining to add to this the dry Greek climate leads to slow growth of the forests and lots of shrubbery. This could give firewood and some base for charcoal manufacturing, but Greece was early dependent on the import of wood for ships and tar.

This meant that the Greeks needed a large merchant navy just to maintain the supply of wood to renew the merchant navy.

The larger ships and galleys needed quality wood to be strong and seaworthy. It is interesting in this connection that the mountains of Lebanon near where the Phoenicians of the Levant arose, where from an early age known for the excellent quality of the cedar trees that grew there lending reason to the Phoenicians having a basis from which to arise as the earliest large naval culture from which the Greeks also learned the craft. They simply had the resources to build the ships at hand. They did not need the ships to import the materials to build the ships. They had it at hand.

The Greeks brought in large amounts of wood for ship building, however. Mostly they had sources of wood in the Balkans to the North and from the Black Sea region meaning they could trade their products for the much-needed lumber.

In exchange the Greeks could trade ceramics, olive oil, wine and metalworks that were highly sought after in those Regions. Again, the

Greeks could trade their manufactured goods for needed raw materials to keep the needed trade going.

Aside from simple crafts most of the more advanced vessels of the Greeks were adapted from the Phoenicians making the maritime technology of the Mediterranean part of the same tradition with the galley as the main type of vessel that was used in ancient times.

This did not mean that there was not a large diversity in the vessels of the Mediterranean world.

From the lowliest raft to the largest trireme, they all had their place in the waters of the Mediterranean.

And exactly the raft along with the hollowed-out tree trunk would be the simplest seacrafts and also remnants of the earliest human seafaring. But just because newer and better vessels are developed does not mean that the originals would not still be in use.

The raft, tree trunk and skin boat would all be used for simple coastal work, the simple crossing and for fishing. Indeed, any situation where the solution just needed to be cheap and simple. Even today the simple raft has its place for crossings and small fishing ventures.

Rafts and skin boats would also be excellent landing vessels for larger ships, when going ashore where the ship could not find harbor or beach. In such situations reaching shore by raft or skin boat would be the way to go.

The raft only needs wood and rope, usually the wood can simply be branches. So, it is easy and fast to build and requires little and can be scaled up as needed.

The skin boat requires more skill to make; a frame from thin wood or branches and the skin then needs to be fitted on to it.

A hollowed-out tree trunk is extremely sturdy, but requires a large tree trunk and a lot of work to finish. Making them less likely when other options are available.

Going on from these options we arrive at actual boats made from planks. The basic version of these would be classic boat shapes that would be rowed or in larger cases have a small sail. This is the classic rowboat type that has lasted through the ages. These would be used for fishing, short distance transport and notably to sail out to larger ships to bring back cargo, if the larger ships could not go to shore.

We now come to the larger vessels that were of a more advanced technology. The large vessels of the Mediterranean world of the ancient Greeks were based on the galley class ships.

THE GALLEY

A galley is at its core a heavily enlarged rowboat with the option of adding a mast and sail, but the main propulsion is oars when conditions are not right for simple square rigging.

The galley is thought to have originated in Egypt during the old kingdom between 2700-2280 BC. From there it spread up the Levantine coast to the Phoenicians and further along the coast of Anatolia to the Minoan Greeks and later passed on to the Mycenaean Greeks.

The galley had thus become common across the Mediterranean during the bronze age and became the dominant large ship type throughout antiquity.

This does make sense as the galley is an excellent ship for the conditions of the Mediterranean.

The combination of oars and sail for propulsion meant that it would both go anywhere by rowing, but also could take advantage of the regular onshore and offshore winds common to the Mediterranean.

The gallery came to sport a huge variety of the basic design, but always had a low freeboard to allow for rowers and oars.

It would also usually be long and slender to allow for easy passing through the water and for more rowers along the length of the ship. This does have variation depending on the purpose of the vessel, however. A cargo ship would have more width to allow for more cargo, while a warship would be longer and narrower to allow for more crew and speed.

A cargo ship would also rely much more on wind power than a warship to reduce the need for manpower.

It is a common trait for cargo ships to be bulkier than warships of the same general type all throughout history, but the galley type is probably the first time that the distinction started to develop and not until late in its development.

This is due to the galley for the first long part of its history being a combined cargo and warship.

It does make sense that cargo ships were also warships, when we consider the way of the Mediterranean world of the time.

The borders of the ancient cultures were diffuse and help was far away, when venturing out, so any vessel going far from home would need to be able to fend for itself and really be a self-supporting community in and of itself, so a large armed crew would be needed.

This meant that there would also always be manpower to man the oars although only with the advent of specialized war galleys would the crew be so large that it could be rowed at very significant speeds.

Great speed was not that important in the early days, however, since it was not until the introduction of the ram as a naval weapon that speed and maneuverability became paramount.

Before the ram naval combat was simply hand combat fought aboard the ships. The ships would sail up to each other and board each other engaging in hand-to-hand combat until one side was defeated meaning that there was little difference between naval and land combat.

So, a ship would basically be a small tribe armed and, on the move, which also meant that people on land would be apprehensive about ships coming near. There was little difference between traders and marauders. They could quickly become one or the other.

This adds to the reasoning behind establishing daughter cities. One galley brought along what amounted to a small community of armed men, who were at the same time not specialized soldiers. They had a craft meaning they could establish a community, where they arrived and by establishing a community, they could gain the trust of the tribes living nearby making it possible for the mother city to trade with people, who would otherwise not trust them.

Add to this that the community that would be the crew of a galley would be a band of brothers. That is, they would be exclusively male. This meant that they would intermarry with the daughters of the local tribes creating a mixed society.

Even though this intermarrying would not always happen voluntarily it did mean that a relationship was established and it is often easier to do business with the father of your grandchild than with a complete stranger, because there is a relationship.

The important thing to remember about the trade of old is that the vessel once it left the home port would become a society unto itself with no way of communicating with the mother city and they would often be gone to a long time cementing the crew as a society unto itself making it far easier for them to settle a new place simply because the ship had become their home and it would itself be the original nexus of the daughter city. After all, the crew lived, worked, ate and slept aboard.

The ancient society was based around the oikos, the household or tribal economy, so trust was based on filial relationships, so trade would also be based on the establishment of functioning relationships between families, clans and tribes.

A galley was one of the largest investments that could be made ranging alongside buildings, but the gallery was a moving machine that would leave the homeland unlike buildings. It was a significant investment that would need to be made by the wealthy families of the mother city. What was then important would be that the chieftains of those families would need that investment to be entrusted to someone.

This would usually be to the sons of these chieftains, who would become leaders of the galley crews with poorer families supplying the crewmembers.

As such whenever there would be a surplus of sons with only the eldest able to directly inherit the fathers giving younger sons the option of manning a galley and seeking their fortune elsewhere would be an efficient way of averting conflict at home and through the daughter city / Mother city relationship positive contact could afterwards be maintained.

This meant that the financing of a galley could be a way to give younger sons some form of inheritance and the possibility of establishing themselves rather than becoming destitute at home.

This is not that different from the reasoning behind the great migration from Europe to the Americas, where those who had little to hope for in the homeland went to America to find a better lot for themselves.

The Greeks did something similar and in doing so established an efficient trade network built on the relationship between those who set out and those who stayed behind. And by also being a means of gaining much needed supplies to the mother city it served multiple purposes.

The galleys used for this purpose were not exactly luxurious, but it was not a society of great luxury.

The earliest galleys shared the defining features that all later galleys would share. They had a small draught; that is very little of the vessel was submerged in the water making it skit over the water. The freeboard or height of the railing above the water was kept low to give the rowers better efficiency in rowing. This had the disadvantage of making it less seaworthy in rough weather, but since galleys usually do not use ballast, they would stay afloat even when heavily damaged. This meant that they very rarely sank.

The earliest galleys lacked a keel so they were fitted with an internal rigging between bow and stern due to the lack of stiffness along the length of the ship. This prevented hogging or bending at the middle of the galley's length.

A keel would be developed by the time of Greek expansion, but they did maintain internal rigging to help keep the hull stiff on the waves.

This rigging was also part of the system around the mast, as the masts of the galleys would be raised or lowered depending on whether the sail were to be used.

This all meant that the rigging, mast and sail could be raised and lowered depending on whether it was advantageous or would hamper the efficiency of the rowers.

Steering was done either by coordinating the rowers on either side or by the use of the two steering oars on either side of the stern.

The galley would be long and slender both to cut well through the water, but also to fit as many rowers as possible along the sides. This limited the rowing capacity as the galley needed to be longer and longer to get more rowers, but there was a limit to length and stability of the design.

This would later be remedied by having more levels of rowers as seen with the bireme with two levels of rowers that started to appear in the 8th century BC.

But until then galleys only had one level of rowers thus limiting the muscle power that could be available and thus also the size and weight of the ship.

The construction of the hull would be mortise and tenon technique giving it a form of stitched construction between the planks. The built or fitting together of the planks would be carvel built, which remained the dominant built on the Mediterranean until steel hulls arrived. This is in contrast to the clinker built of Northern Europe

The one leveled galley that the Greeks used until the advent of the bireme would mostly be either triaconters or penteconters. That is thirty or fifty oared ships. 15 or 25 on either side.

THE TRIACONTER

Triaconter literally means "thirty oared" referring directly to how many oars were used to propel it through the water. This also signifies that it would have a crew of at least 30 men. One to each oar.

The triaconter is one of the ship numbers mentioned in Homer's Iliad. Other numbers are mentioned and some are more prestigious, but a number of 30 men, who would be armed make for a good unit size.

So, a triaconter can be said to refer to a floating contingent of 30 men with all the combat or work power that this entails.

A chieftain of a triaconter would be medium/small given his number of men. The triaconter would have been a fairly common ship type that would have served as both a small warship and cargo ship.

The triaconter would most likely have been used for short distance trade and contact. It would have been efficient and not too costly to set out with.

It would have been seaworthy and could go far because its crew was large enough for distant travel and the size of the ship was enough to have a reasonable cargo.

This would mean that the Aegean Sea and Ionian Sea would have seen many triaconters on their waves going to and from mainland Greece.

Given that the triaconter is mentioned in the Iliad It would at least have been common in the dark age between the end of the bronze age and the beginning of the classical age.

It is however most likely that the triaconters and similar had also been common during the bronze age in the period where the Iliad is set.

This fits with the naval activity of both the Mycenaean Greeks, Minoans, Phoenicians and Egyptians, who all traveled far in the Mediterranean during the bronze age.

This would also be reasonable as the triaconter along with the larger penteconter would be the main vessel used during the Greek expansion during the 8th to 5th century BC.

The triaconter would be one masted with only a partial deck and a rather open structure as more complex superstructures would only appear with the bireme This structure was again shared with the penteconter that was more or less a larger version of the triaconter.

THE PENTECONTER

As the triaconter had 30 oars the penteconter literally means 50 oars making it somewhat larger than the triaconter.

The penteconter was the size of the galley of a more important chieftain. In the Iliad and Odyssey of Homer the penteconter is the ship size of Odysseus and it is also the size of the Argo of Jason and the Argonauts.

This also shows that this ship size is where it becomes a fully self-sufficient tribe that can journey far and take on many adventures on its own. Jason led the Argo and its crew far into the Black Sea and Odysseus traveled all over the Mediterranean.

The penteconter would thus be a likely type used for traveling out to less known areas to establish new trade connections and trading posts as the crew was so large that it could take on the dangers that it might encounter.

Other oar numbers than 30 and 50 existed and are mentioned, but there seem to be the most common types.

The penteconter would thus likely have been a common sight across the Mediterranean with both Greeks and Phoenicians using it.

Aside from the number of oars and thus length the penteconter would not have been different from the triaconter. The build would have been the same.

The penteconter would be both a commercial and military vessel depending on the situation. It was able to work both independently and as part of a fleet as described in the Iliad.

It's at capacity for real naval strategy was very limited, however, as it like the smaller triaconter thought by simply closing in on other vessels and boarding it essentially making naval combat identical to land combat except that it was done on enclosed floating platforms.

This meant that the ability for naval strategy was at the time of the penteconter very limited. The penteconter was still an unspecialized ship.

The fact that the penteconter had only a single row of rowers on each side meant that the force that it could gain from speed was limited.

It would reach reasonable speeds of up to 10 knots, but more averagely 5-7 knots, but this speed did not add up to much ramming force.

Real ramming force and muscle would only come about with the development of the bireme, which had two levels of rovers on each side doubling the force that could be brought about.

It was the penteconter that would serve as the basis of the bireme, however, as it was the length were the structural pros and cons of more oars to length leveled out. Making it longer to add more rowers was possible and was done as galleys up to 120 rowers are mentioned in the Iliad, but it did make these galleys less structurally strong.

The solution to wanting extra manpower from more rowers while keeping the structural stability of a shorter length, which also had the added benefit of a shorter tuning radius was to add an extra level of rowers to the penteconter.

This would be the bireme.

THE BIREME

The bireme started to develop among the Phoenicians 700-800 BC and quickly spread to the Greeks.

The name bireme comes from Latin biremis (two oars, in Greek it was called dieres).

In naval technology the bireme was a significant step up. Its two levels of rowers on either side meant that the available muscle power of the galley was increased significantly. It meant that much more force would be had to the unit of length giving an advantage in maneuverability as a shorter ship turns faster.

A bireme was not necessarily faster than a penteconter, but this was not the point. The extra row of rower most importantly greatly increased the mass that could be moved. Thus, the bireme could be much heavier and carry far more load.

This stepped in well with the development of the ram as a naval weapon. The ram had appeared as a naval weapon at around 1000 BC. On the penteconter it could mainly be used to attack the oars of other vessels, but to be a truly effective weapon against the hull of another ship, it needed to have a lot of weight behind it aside from its speed.

This necessitated far more muscle to drive forth the ram.

Furthermore, ballast would be added in the form of stones at the bottom of the hull to increase the weight that the ram would hit with at speed. Again, more weight, more muscle.

The ram would be a bronze clad fist of wood mounted at the bow of the bireme. It would not be a continuation of the keel, but be mounted onto the hull. This was to make it possible for it to break off if locked in another ship rather than break the keel, if too much stress was added. Then only the ram rather than the entire ship would be lost.

The ramming tactic significantly changed how naval battles were fought. It became an age of larger fleets rather than lone ships.

This led to the development of specialized naval tactics, where the fleets tried to outmaneuver each other to come into ramming position. This meant that the bireme also needed to be maneuverable to be able to turn quickly, which necessitated the ships being shorter. The multiple levels of rowers allowed for the biremes to be shorter than its one leveled predecessor and thus much more maneuverable.

The bireme was also much more technically complex showing the significant maturing of the city states that built them. This was no longer the simple galley built by extended families, but were the advanced crafts built by a more complex and affluent society.

This really owed to the Greek trade network in the Mediterranean established before. It allowed the city states to gain the resources they needed through trade and to build efficient export industries that further added to the affluence of the city states.

What then became paramount was the maintaining of the connection to the daughter cities and the valuable exchange that this offered.

In order to maintain and protect these connections fleets were built to patrol and secure the trade routes.

This developed into a significant specialization of ships being built for specific purposes other than being all around crafts that could be both for combat and trade.

The bireme with many rowers would mainly evolve into a combat vessel although cargo and trade vessels would also have two levels of rowers just significantly fewer than military vessels.

There would thus come about a split in ship development with the military bireme evolving into the trireme with no less than three levels of rowers, while the cargo type would be increasingly focused on being propelled by the sail and develop into the Kerkouroi, which became large grain carriers. They still had rovers, but only about ten on each side for a standard sized vessel. It relied more on sails and the wind and most importantly since it was not a combat vessel, it neither needed to be fast or maneuverable.

The bireme thus became the type from which significant specialization stemmed with more advanced societies building ships that were built for specific purposes.

This is the vessel that led into the classical age, where the Greek Mediterranean world had been established and became more systematic in its trade networks.

As this continued the competition between the city states for dominance intensified and also the competition with the Phoenicians now under Persian rule and the Phoenician daughter city of Carthage in the west in today's Tunisia.

This led to a naval arms race that led to the development of the famed trireme. The ultimate combat ship of antiquity.

THE TRIREME

The trireme was the ultimate development of the ram-based warship. Although the Carthaginians and Romans developed quadriremes and quinqueremes with more rows the trireme would be the final version, where it was an actual added row of oarsmen.

The trireme thus also became a symbol of the naval power of classical antiquity. This was the ship type that the Athenians invested in to establish their great navy, which defeated the Phoenician based Persian navy at Salamis and thus cemented the Greek rule of the sea.

The trireme was not longer than the bireme, but had an extra third level of rowers. It was rowed with between 30 and 50 oars on each level of rowers.

A basic trireme would sport a crew of about 200 men; 170 rowers, 13 sailors, 10 soldiers and some officers. The hoplite soldiers would man the upper deck to protect from boarding, the trireme came side by side with an enemy ship. This was not the goal, however, as the main attack was the ram, which acquired massive force from the large number of oarsmen on the trireme.

The oarsmen on the Athenian and other Greek triremes were not slaves, but free citizens of the city state, who could not afford the cost of hoplite armor and thus served as oarsmen instead.

Thus, the trireme also served to equalize and democratize the city state as the poorer citizens became just as important in the navy as the more affluent.

Although the trireme was so heavily based on rowing it did have a mast and sail, which could be raised through advanced internal rigging, when the conditions were right and lowered again, when it was going to combat, where a raised mast would be a hindrance. The sail would thus be used to give the rowers a rest under the right conditions. The right conditions were wind to stern as the trireme and other galleys did not lie deep in the water and had limited maneuverability in the wind. When under sail it was steered by two large oars by the stern.

The importance of the rowers on the trireme greatly added to the democratization of Greek and especially Athenian culture as it allowed the lower classes an important role in defense and maintenance of naval presence. One could thus argue that much of what we equate with classical Greek culture and politics thus takes its roots on the decks of the triremes, because they were so manpower intensive.

And that is a great point that when something important is labor intensive and the laborers needed, they can gain more of a say in society rather than when labor is less needed. The navy of the triremes was labor intensive!

The size and complexity of the trireme also necessitated a much more advanced society which differentiates the Archaic era of colonization from the classical era of consolidation. The colonization effort in the Mediterranean ebbed out in the classical period with the societies becoming more complex instead and those who left, did so to the older and more urbanized regions of the near east instead.

Ironically, they thus started to go to the very region of the Persian empire that they used the trireme to resist. This development was the classical forerunner to the Hellenistic period, where much of the antique middle east would be heavily Hellenized and would remain so all the way into the heavily Hellenistic Eastern Roman empire.

The trireme thus filled out a historical and societal niche in a period, where ocean trade needed to be protected from other similarly advanced societies.

It thus should not come as a surprise that the trireme and indeed all large combat galleys would die out as the Romans secured the Mediterranean as a peaceful Mare Internum. At that time smaller and more numerous patrol vessels of the Liburna type were used to combat remaining piracy.

Furthermore, the Romans also ended the age of Naval ramming tactics as they developed efficient boarding bridges, which again brought more land-based tactics to the seas.

The trireme thus had a niche heavily associated with classical Greece where its skilled manpower intensive design led it to profoundly affect how society developed in the city states.

But the large size of naval combat vessels could only come about because of the increased need to protect the sea-lanes. After all it makes no sense to invest in large naval vessels, if you do not have something valuable for them to protect and it was not only about protecting the homeland from attack.

It was to protect a heavily developed trade network to the daughter cities and overseas trade partners that had expanded rapidly into the classical era.

This advancement in trade and the large need for bulk materials of the Greek city states meant that the cargo vessels had equally expanded in size just like the much better-known triremes.

These large cargo vessels were the Kerkouroi!

THE KERKOUROS

The Kerkouros was the largest cargo and merchant ship of classical antiquity. Like the trireme it was a development from the simple galley, but it had moved in a different direction, it was not built for speed or maneuverability. It was built for cargo capacity.

When Athens received its large deliveries of grain from the areas north of the Black Sea, it would be on kerkouroi. A situation that would persist into the Greek Eastern Roman empire and lead to the heavy influence of Greek Eastern Roman culture and Orthodox Christianity on the Eastern Slavs of Ukraine and Russia.

The kerkouroi were very large merchant ships for their time owing to them being large bulk carriers of grain and other raw materials to Greece.

They were slow and although they also used rowers like all other galleys. They only had a small single row on each side. It did not need to go fast, but needed to save on manpower cost. It also had a sail and used it much more than the biremes or triremes. It was not more maneuverable under the wind, but could afford the wait as long as the cargo reached home in the end.

The kerkouroi became very large with a cargo capacity of between 250 and 500 tons, which was impressive for the time.

These were basically the container ships of antiquity and their containers were the amphora made in a huge variety of shapes and sizes to transport the many different products of trade like olive oil exported from Greece and grain imported back. The amphora would be manufactured in the Greek exporting city and the daughter city at the other end would produce the amphora for the import as the same amphora could not always be used for different products.

Especially olive oil ruined the amphora after use.

The amphorae were loaded into racks designed for their pointed ends and bound together securing them in the cargo hold of the kerkouroi. The handles on either side of the amphora made them excellent for carrying between two people for easy manual loading and unloading.

Thus, the hold of the kerkouros could be easily filled and emptied, which is a boon for bulk cargo with limited value to weight.

The large cargo capacity and limited crew of the kerkouros due to the sail and ease of loading with the amphora meant that Greece could through its seafaring activity support a much larger population than the land itself could sustain.

Thus, in many ways the kerkouros much more than the trireme was the real symbol of classical Greek seafaring, because it enabled the city states to support larger populations, which again led to the population surplus that could spread Hellenism through the orient as this population surplus naturally would not be engaged in agriculture. They could engage in mercenary activity and sail off to other lands to seek the fortune lacking in the homeland.

None of this would have been possible without an efficient bulk carrier like the Kerkouros.

Thus, everything about classical Greece necessitated the Greeks to be enterprising seafaring people simply, because their culture could not sustain itself without the stable foods imported on large vessels like the kerkouroi.

Before the advent of these large transport vessels the city states instead needed to expel excess population that could not be fed by the available food.

This in turn meant that a network of related daughter cities would be established from where foodstuff would later be imported on vessels like the Kerkouros.

CONCLUSION

The main answer and conclusion to this little book is that the Greeks became a seafaring people due to a process that had as its onset the physical characteristics of Greece itself. There simply is much access to the sea and the sea provided an easier path to transport than the land.

This cannot stand alone, however, as what also made the Greeks seek to the sea was the opportunity that was across the sea. The increased scarcity that presented itself in Greece at the onset of the iron age meant that there was something to be acquired by traveling across the sea. Either through trade that brought goods back or through immigration where people sought out greener pastures.

Another element that increased seafaring and the establishment of colonies by the Greeks was also the particular societal structure of iron age Greece, where the Greeks retreated into competitive city states that did not readily cooperate.

This contracts to the larger bronze age kingdoms that could better even out surplus and deficit across a larger area. This can be shown through the reading of the Iliad, where King Agamemnon could drum up a larger army fleet, which would not be possible again until the city state leagues of classical Greece.

The early iron age city states could only rely on their local land and what could be brought across the sea through trade. This harsh environment led to the large-scale colonization of the archaic era, where the Greek colonies across the Mediterranean and Black Sea rim were established.

This gave the city states the extra land for daughter cities that was not available in Greece proper. So, the Greeks took to the sea, because they lacked the extra room for expansion of economic activity at home.

Yet a further reason is the timing of the archaic colonial expansion. It took place at a time where much of the coastline of the Mediterranean had the room for establishment of colonies that were often welcomed by local rulers, because it gave access to trade in foreign goods.

What finally made the difference in making the Greeks into a truly seafaring people was the development from the end of the large bronze age kingdoms into the city states of the archaic iron age. This is where the Greeks sent out a large portion of its excess population that could not be supplied by the city states' capacity.

These immigrants went out in smaller groups in triaconters and penteconters numbering the crews of these.

A very good image of these small bands can be had again from the bronze age epics of the Iliad and Odyssey, where the men travel in exactly these boat types that remained into the early iron age. Thus, I can only advise that to get an idea of these boat crews and the conditions they had, then you should read these epics.

Through these early immigrations the structure of daughter cities that made the foundation of Greek seafaring during the classical era was established. This made it possible for the city states of the classical era to be supplied with basic goods and thus retain a larger population and grow a larger more diverse naval presence.

Thus, the triaconters and penteconters that were all around vessels evolved into the more specialized biremes and triremes for combat and the Kerkouros for bulk trade.

Thus, the immigration of the archaic era set the stage for the much more evolved seafaring of the classical era.

The evolution of the Greeks into the seafaring people that they became is thus heavily dependent on first the layout of the country itself, but what made them become truly seafaring outside their home land and the well-known kingdoms of the levant, was the competition and small secluded size of the city states. The relative isolation of the city states from each other and the fact that they blocked further evolution at home meant that opportunity and new land and resources needed to be found across the sea.

This development reached its peak in the classical era, where this expanded network of sea-oriented cities created an international trade network that allowed the city states to fight far above their weight class.

This was a centuries long development that started with the end of the bronze age kingdoms and ended with the highly connected civilization of the Hellenistic period that would form the seaward backbone of the Mediterranean as the inner sea of the Roman Empire.